GRACE

ON THE

GO

Quick Prayers for Determined Dieters

BARBARA BARTOCCI

MOREHOUSE PUBLISHING

An imprint of Church Publishing Incorporated
Harrisburg—New York

Unless otherwise noted, the Scripture quotations contained herein are from the New Revised Standard Version Bible, copyright © 1989 by the Division of Christian Education of the National Council of Churches of Christ in the U.S.A. Used by permission. All rights reserved.

Morehouse Publishing, 4775 Linglestown Road, Harrisburg, PA 17105

Morehouse Publishing, 445 Fifth Avenue, New York, NY 10016

Morehouse Publishing is an imprint of Church Publishing Incorporated.

Cover art: Ablestock

Cover design by Jennifer Glosser

Library of Congress Cataloging-in-Publication Data
Bartocci, Barbara.
  Grace on the go : quick prayers for determined dieters / by Barbara Bartocci.
    p. cm.
  ISBN 978-0-8192-2287-9 (pbk.)
  1. Dieters—Prayers and devotions. I. Title.
BV4596.D53B37 2008
242'.86—dc22

                                    2007051496

Printed in the United States of America

08 09 10 11 12 13   10 9 8 7 6 5 4 3 2 1

Other books in the Grace on the Go series
Grace on the Go: Quick Prayers for Compassionate Caregivers
Grace on the Go: Quick Prayers for New Moms
Grace on the Go: 101 Quick Ways to Pray

Reviewers' comments about
Grace on the Go: 101 Quick Ways to Pray

"A gem in the everyday spirituality genre with its wide-ranging examples of how we can make every moment a devotional one." *Spirituality and Practice*

"This new book from award-winning author Barbara Bartocci has breathed fresh air and energy into my prayer life." Lisa Hendey, reviewer, Catholicmom.net

"A fine little book that uses everyday situations as cues for prayers." *The Lutheran*

"A best-selling author tells how to find God in the midst of life's commotion and busyness." Canadian monthly, *Faith and Friends*

An excerpt from *Grace on the Go: 101 Quick Ways to Pray* is one of the "Top Ten" on *www.Beliefnet.com*

". . . wonderful ways to incorporate prayer and God's peace into our busy days." Jane Pitt, mother of actor Brad Pitt

Re: other books from the award-winning author

Paradise
was very nice
for Adam and his madam,
until they filched the fruit and took the fall.
They lost their place
and fell from grace
and you can bet we can't forget
that eating *is the oldest sin of all.*
　　—Victor Buono, *Heavy*

CONTENTS

⸻

INTRODUCTION
TACKLING A WEIGHTY SUBJECT

My first memory of worrying about weight goes back to sixth grade. I was big-boned and tall for my age, and one of my aunts, who hadn't seen me in a few years, said, "My, but she's a *sturdy* little girl, isn't she?" Sturdy? I crept into my bedroom and looked in the mirror. And it was as if I had suddenly ballooned. Wasn't sturdy just another name for . . . fat?

Today when I look at pictures of myself in sixth grade, I see a pretty little girl, neither fat nor thin. But from age eleven on, I began to worry about weight. Body image has been an issue for me.

And an even bigger issue has been my relationship with food.

Food. Wonderful, glorious, mouth-watering food. Food has given me comfort when I'm feeling down. I nibble when I'm anxious or nervous about work. I indulge in gourmet delights to celebrate achievements. I binge on ice cream or chocolate when stressed. And if I'm hurried and hungry, I snack on fast food.

Sound familiar? I know I'm not alone in my struggle. We obsess about food and body image in this country. *Every month* the covers of women's magazines highlight dieting. And don't you just love the way recipes and full-color photos of rich chocolate desserts are displayed on the very next page?

Diet books are best sellers. And even as Americans do get heavier—187 million of us are overweight, which is more than half our population—we compare ourselves to runway models and Hollywood stars that are so thin they look anorexic.

For years, I've yo-yoed my way through diets. Fad diets. Liquid diets. Supervised diets. Grapefruit diets. Protein diets. Good diets. I reach a goal weight, and then life gets turbulent, a food craving takes over—and I'm yo-yoing again. It's a constant battle with "the last ten pounds."

A WEIGHTY SPIRITUAL ISSUE

For years I have consciously tried to walk a spiritual path, making prayer an integral part of my life, reading Scripture daily, asking for the grace I need to live according to God's will.

A while ago, I really got down on myself because I couldn't seem to control my emotional eating. Then one morning, during my prayer time, I realized I had never involved God in my lifelong struggles with food. I had felt embarrassed before God about my lack of willpower around food (as if the Creator didn't already know!), and I had made an assumption that my struggles with food had nothing to do with my spiritual life.

Yet Scripture says we are made in God's image and that our bodies are temples of the spirit. Aren't all of us mind-body-spirit? Maybe it was time to ask: "How am I treating God's temple?"

There are also many Scriptural references to the word *repent*. Jesus told his disciples to repent. And earlier, in Jeremiah: "The Lord says if you repent I will restore you that you may serve me" (Jeremiah 15:19).[1]

A modern interpretation of the word *repent* is "rethink." Cognitive psychologists have learned that by changing unhealthy thinking patterns, people have been able to recover from depression, rebuild self-esteem, release anger, retrieve damaged relationships, and even recuperate from addictive behavior.

Wasn't my eating behavior a little, well, addictive? What would happen, I wondered, if I began to *rethink* my relationship to food and body image, and turned them into an integral part of my spiritual journey? As I thought about this some more, I felt a little thrill.

"Whatever you ask for in prayer, believe that you have received it and it will be yours," Jesus said (Mark 11:24). And, "I can do all things through him who strengthens me," said Paul (Philippians 4:13).

What a joy it would be to embark on a path of more conscious eating. What if food stopped being an emotional crutch and, instead, became a healthy way to nurture God's temple? How freeing to feel at home in my body.

Right then and there, I took a deep breath, and said out loud, "Lord, I repent."

I choose to rethink the way I eat.

Prayerful support to do the same is what *Grace on the Go* offers you. It's small enough to tuck into your purse or pocket, and I hope you will take it with you so you can turn to a meaningful prayer when a food temptation comes—as it will—or you're not sure you can hang in there with your new, healthier way of eating.

In the situations and prayers you read, you'll find quotes from Scripture, from spiritual writers through the ages, and from others who are just like you and me.

Jesus said, "I am the bread of life. Whoever comes to me will never be hungry, and whoever believes in me will never be thirsty" (John 6:35).

This doesn't guarantee that we will never be hungry or thirsty physically, but it is Christ's promise that the "bread of life" will strengthen us to undergo the kind of transformation Paul wrote about in Romans 12:2: "Do not conform any longer to the pattern of this world, but be transformed by the renewing of your mind."[2]

That's what this book is all about. Transforming ourselves, body and soul.

Chapter One
The Media Made Me Do It

"*My body is a temple, with ample parking in the rear.*"

—*Daniel Worona*

Before we begin transforming ourselves, let's look at where we are right now. Ever wondered how much of a hand the media has had in how we think about ourselves and our bodies? Take a look at these statistics.

- Did you know that 40 percent of nine-year-old girls say they've already tried to lose weight?

- Or that 78 percent of seventeen-year-old girls say they dislike their bodies?

- It gets worse: 80 percent of adult women in North America report being unhappy with their bodies. (Men are more accepting of their bodies, but even that is changing with younger men who want "six-pack" abs.)

- Thirty years ago, top models weighed about 8 percent less than the average woman; today, top models weigh 23 percent less—creating an impossible standard of thinness.

- Even models and actors are not considered beautiful enough: magazine covers, advertisements, and movies use computer alterations and body doubles to create flawless images. A Redbook magazine featuring Julia Roberts used her face but attached it to a younger woman's body. I was happy to learn that she protested.

It's hard not to compare ourselves to these "media gods," (or goddesses) especially when they're so pervasive. In the doctor's office, I pick up a copy of *Glamour*. In line at the supermarket, I thumb through the newest *People* magazine. On TV, on billboards—even online—I see false, idealized images.

A PRAYER BEFORE READING A FASHION MAGAZINE

Oh God, do I feel better or worse after I read this magazine? Do I enjoy its trendy content? Or do I close the pages feeling "lesser than" because I haven't got the body of the fashion models pictured? Give me the wisdom to recognize when images are false and not true to life. Give me the strength to close a book that only makes me feel bad about myself. Amen.

ALL SHAPES AND SIZES

Impossibly thin is so "in." My friend Kayla sighed. "Why wasn't I born when Reubens was painting his full-figured women?" Kayla considers herself fat. It's true, she has a generous body. She can shake her booty. And she shops for D-cups in the lingerie section. But she's not obese. She is just a large woman who is well-endowed. She walks two miles a day five days a week, and easily lifts ten-pound weights. But Kayla is obsessed with what her scale says, and hers says 172 pounds.

According to *Prevention* magazine, model Cindy Crawford is not as skinny as some, but her added weight looks good because she's toned it into muscle. The same article says that a "healthy weight" for a woman her height—5'9")—is anywhere from 129 to 169 pounds. That's a *40-pound spread*! And at either end, a woman could be considered healthy.

At the Cooper Institute in Dallas, where researchers study health and fitness, Dr. Steven Blair argues that society focuses too much on dropping pounds and too little on exercise and being physically fit.

Maybe that's why I like Queen Latifah and actress Kathy Bates. Both stay physically fit, but their bodies are as robust as their talent, and they're not trying to "skinny down." Why can't we acknowledge that beautiful bodies come in all shapes and sizes? And it's *okay*!

A PRAYER FOR THE 1 PERCENT

Oh Lord, scientists say that
The genome code is 99 percent the same
For all human beings.
We differ from one another in only 1 percent.
And yet, what variety spills out of that 1 percent.

Why would I ever let myself be beguiled
Into thinking there is only one size
Or shape or color—or weight—
That counts?
"Glorify God in your body," said the apostle Paul
    (1 Corinthians 6:20).
Yes, Lord, I do.
That's why, in your name,
I want to be as fit as I can be in body, mind, and spirit.
I praise the magnificent multiplicity
That exists in the 1 percent difference.
It reminds me of what I know to be true:
One size does not fit all.

BODY IMAGE

"Body image" isn't connected to what we *actually* look like. It's how we perceive ourselves and our bodies. A false image can prompt a woman with anorexia to see herself as fat when she's at starvation weight. Some cosmetic surgery "junkies" are never satisfied with how they look.

My friend Nora does not have a perfect body. She veers more to plump than to thin. Still, "I don't hear you lapsing into the female whine of 'Gotta go on a diet' or 'I need to lose weight,'" I said. "You seem totally comfortable with yourself. How do you do it?"

She smiled. "Sometimes, when I'm alone and catch a glimpse in the mirror, I wish I were a little slimmer, but mostly, I look at myself holistically: as body, mind, spirit, and soul. When I'm with others, I forget about my body because I'm so involved with the world I'm in. There are too many exciting things to do and people to meet and ideas to discuss for me to let a wish to be slimmer get in the way. I try and eat healthy food. Beyond that, I don't worry about it."

A Prayerful Rumination While Sitting in the Hot Tub at the Ladies' Spa

Oh Lord, I almost didn't step in
When I saw her sitting there.
Look.
Her belly is smooth satin,
Uncreased. Taut.
Unlike mine.
Since my babies,
Mine has a more interesting texture.
Waffle weave,
Herringbone, Cablestitch.
It's as comfortable as an old sweater

Whose pockets sag with treasures.
I need your help, oh Lord, To celebrate
The richness of my belly
Whose fabric is so well worn.

A JOURNEY OF ACCEPTANCE

Self-acceptance doesn't mean you have to stay where you are. Life is a journey, and the very word *journey* implies we *don't* stay in one place.

"But you have to change the way you see yourself *before* you can change the way you look," says Dr. Nick Yphantides. He should know. This preventive-medicine specialist dropped from 467 pounds to 220 pounds with the help of prayer and dieting.

"Forgetting what lies behind and straining foward to what lies ahead, I press on toward the goal," wrote Paul (Philippians 3:13–14).

If we can be healthier by changing certain habits, we should do it—though not because we hate the way we look, but because we love ourselves.

What better prayer than this?

O God
Help me
To believe
The truth about myself
No matter
How beautiful it is![3]

Our bodies are precious gifts and blessings from our Creator. They can help us as we seek the Holy. If we must compare, let us look to the saints, not to the media.

A PRAYER OF YES!

Dear Lord, I say YES!
Yes to loving myself.
I am as you made me.
Unique.
Extraordinary.
Unparalleled.
Dear Lord, I say YES!
Yes to healthy eating
Being active.
Choosing right.
I surrender this area of my life to God.
Dear Lord, I say YES!

CHAPTER TWO
STARTING RIGHT

"Dieting is hard by the yard, but by the inch, it's a cinch."

Does this scene sound familiar? It's the very first day of Diet Number 639. Last night, you ate a stack of Oreos and a huge bowl of chocolate ice cream because "tomorrow I start my diet."

Now the new day has dawned, your heart is pure, your spirit determined, and by gosh, "I'll lose twenty pounds (or fifty pounds or . . . fill in the number) by my high-school reunion" (or "the wedding" or "bathing suit season" or—you choose).

And you do it! But like any good practitioner of yo-yo dieting, once the diet is "over" and the goal achieved, the lure of Oreos and chocolate ice cream returns and the pounds whisper, like sirens of old, "We want to come back, we want to come back."

One day you get on the scales and *voila*! Your old friends—those pounds—have returned. They just can't stay away. Sometimes, they bring a few more friends with them.

A GOOD-BYE PRAYER TO OLD FRIENDS

Good-bye, old friends,
My extra pounds.
God bless.
You have left before and then returned.
But now I say good-bye for good.
I wish you well,
But not on me.

CHANGING HABITS

In the past, one of the biggest reasons I regained weight—and perhaps, you too—is that I didn't permanently change my eating *habits*. Habits—those behaviors we do automatically—can be good things. Time-savers, too. (Wouldn't you hate to have to realize every single morning that you should brush your teeth and then figure out how to do it?)

But changing *poor* habits is difficult because we so easily return to automatic behavior. It takes a great deal of effort to, first, notice habitual behavior and, second, to change it.

I've heard more than one person say, always with an accompanying sigh, "I guess I lack self-control. I always wind up giving in." I've said those very words myself. Then I came across this observation from the authors of *Free to Be Thin*: "Do you get out of bed when your alarm goes off? Arrive at work on time? Answer your phone when it rings? Pay your bills on time? Make decisions? If you answer yes to any of these questions, you have plenty of self-control. You're just using it selectively."

Selective self-control.

That hit home with me.

It also gave me hope because it reminded me that I *do* have self-control. I'm very self-disciplined in areas that are important to me. So, apparently, part of me didn't see it as important to change my eating habits for *good*. I opted for short-term solutions (the latest diet) instead of long-term change.

A PRAYER FOR SELF-CONTROL

Almighty God,
Your will for me is health in body, mind, and soul.
Inspire me now with self-control
And the discipline I need
To free myself forever from food addictions and
Unhealthy eating.
I know I cannot do it by my will alone.
So in confidence, I pray,

Let your will be done in me.
Through Jesus Christ our Lord. Amen.

In order to change our eating habits for good, we have to understand what's behind the way we eat now. Anyone truly interested in long-term change needs to ponder these questions:

- What purpose does overeating serve in my life?
- When I'm feeling "empty" inside, do I fill my emptiness with food?
- What kinds of food do I crave?
- How does food pacify my tension, stress or frustration? Or my loneliness, anger or insecurity?
- Am I able to recognize real hunger? Or does it get mixed up with psychological or spiritual hunger?

A Prayer of Encouragement

Oh Lord, I am encouraged by these words: "Long standing habits will resist but they will be vanquished in time by a better habit if you persevere! The flesh will cry out but will be restrained by the spirit."[4]

Conscious Living, Unconscious Eating?

Living consciously is what Jesus asked of his disciples.

Many times, he encouraged his followers to become more aware. "Stay awake!" he said. "Stay awake and pray that you may not come into the time of trial." And he acknowledged their human limitations by adding, "The spirit is indeed willing, but the flesh is weak" (Matthew 26:41).

Conscious *watching* means we pay attention to our behavior and to our inner motivations in order to learn what's really going on inside us.

FIRST PRAYERFUL ACTION: START A FOOD JOURNAL

- *What* do I eat?
- *When* do I eat it?
- *Why* do I eat it?

A food journal lets us practice Jesus' admonition to *watch*.

My first food journal, a little spiral-bound notebook, had a red cover. Red symbolizes the Holy Spirit, and I wanted God's spirit to be with me.

For three weeks, I wrote down everything I ate and when and why. A good admonition is this one: "If you bite it, write it."

In the beginning, don't try to control what you eat. Just *notice*.

A FOOD JOURNAL PRAYER

In the name of Jesus Christ
Who celebrated the bounty of food and wine, and
Who told his disciples to "Watch!" and to "Pray!"
I commit to keeping this daily food diary.

Keep me honest in my observations.
Help me to see patterns.
Deliver me from temptations. Amen.

One of my food journal entries—for a Sunday in October—read:

8 a.m. 1 serving oatmeal, 1 cup strawberries, 1 cup sugar-free cocoa

Noon salad (lettuce, onion, dried cranberries, cucumber slices, zucchini slices, fat-free dressing), 3 Wasa crackers, light Velveeta cheese, 1 non-fat yogurt

Mid-afternoon 1 pear, 1 apple

Dinner 4 oz. steak, fresh mushrooms and spinach cooked in 1 tsp olive oil, plus green tossed salad

So far, so good. And then . . . *uh-oh*.

Later that night, I ate an entire stack of Ritz crackers, another cup of yogurt, 2 pieces of chocolate, and a second whole stack of Ritz crackers.

This was binge behavior. What was I feeling? I wrote: "Very nervous about meeting my deadline for an article. Writing not going well. Took time off to read a magazine while I ate the Ritz crackers. Wanted to continue reading. In my mind, the two are habitually connected: as long as I'm eating, I'm allowed to read. So I kept eating the crackers. Why was I reading? Avoidance behavior: trying to avoid my work."

A food journal helps identify precarious emotional situations and the kinds of foods that make you shout, "Gotta have it! Now!" Once you understand more about your eating patterns and your personal "danger" foods, you'll be able to more wisely decide on one of three alternatives.

Avoidance: Should you remove a food totally from your diet?

Moderation: Should you consume a certain food very, very carefully?

Substitution: Should you find a healthier food that fulfills your need? Or an action you can do instead of eating?

I decided I was better off treating ice cream the way an alcoholic treats booze: I avoid it. I never eat it—*ever*—and haven't for five years. As long as I don't eat *any*, I don't crave it.

A more moderate solution would be to limit yourself to a low-fat ice cream bar instead of opening a half-gallon of ice cream, or to eat a single piece of Dove's dark chocolate instead of a whole candy bar.

Working in an at-home office as I do makes it easy to wander out to my kitchen. And then—on it goes: the light inside my refrigerator.

As I tried to figure out an action alternative, I remembered two eight-pound hand weights gathering dust in my closet. My food journal showed me that when I'm physically active, I'm less likely to eat inappropriately. So I started lifting the weights when I felt a snack attack coming on. A secondary benefit? Friends are starting to say, "You've got great arms."

FIRE DRILL!

Don, who weighed 260 pounds but was able to shrink to 198 over a two-year period, calls it his "Fire Drill." When he feels a food craving coming on, he immediately drinks 8 ounces of water to help fill him. Then he goes for a 10-minute fast walk, and while he walks he pulls out his prayer beads.

He said having a plan in place for a food craving moment is like practicing what you'll do in case of fire. If a real fire breaks out, you won't panic because your actions are programmed in advance.

His prayer is simple and repetitive:

Oh God, Free me from temptation.
Thou—master me.
God, free me from temptation.
Thou—master me.

An even easier prayer is this one: *"Help me, help me, help me."*

ANOTHER PRAYER WHEN A CRAVING HITS

Oh beloved Lord,
My soul hungers and thirsts for you.
Yet at this moment, another hunger stirs.

I know this craving to be a false god,
And I want to face it down
As Jesus faced down
His tempter in the desert.
But its powerful tentacles
Have wrapped around me.
Alone, I'm not strong enough to wrestle free.
Humbly, I throw myself on your Divine mercy,
Be with me now, I pray.

SECOND PRAYERFUL ACTION: NAME THE DANGEROUS FOODS AND SITUATIONS FOR *YOU*

"Naming" is a powerful spiritual tool. In Scripture, Abram was renamed Abraham to signify his willingness to follow God's call. Simon became Peter. Saul became Paul. In all cases, it signified a *change in consciousness*.

How can you use naming in your diet?

A PRAYER OF NAMING

Oh Lord, another name for food
Is fuel.
It powers my body, a precious vehicle of God.
Help me accept food's role and true name.
Help me eat only what I need—and no more.
Free me from using food to satisfy non-physical hungers.
And thank you, God, for the blessing of
Having adequate fuel for my body.

We can't fix a problem until we correctly identify it. By accurately *naming* the situations that prompt cravings and bring on food binges, you are taking a big step toward permanent change.

For instance, Ashley realized, "What pushes my button is when someone treats me unfairly."

Feeling unloved did it to Jessica.

"Boredom!" shouted Amanda, an outgoing, energetic extrovert.

Naming our danger zones takes a little time. I'm still discovering new situations to name. But more awareness of the way food and emotions connect for *you* can help shift your eating patterns. Self-knowledge will also take you farther along on your spiritual path.

I love this quote by Thomas Merton: "Sanctity is nothing more than becoming ourselves. Pray for the grace to be committed to the vocation God has given you to be yourself."

Yes! Pray to be yourself—free of food's siren song.

We can also enhance our prayers, according to author Edward Hays, by being creative in the way we address God. For instance,

Oh Beautiful God Who Has Made All in Your Image, remind me to whisper, when I look in a mirror, "I am loved and made beautiful by the Creator."

Oh My Divine Source of Health and Wellness, encourage me today to eat in moderation and make time for exercise.

Oh My God, the Ever-Patient, save me from my impatience to lose weight faster than a slow but healthy two pounds a week. When I occasionally plateau, keep me faithful to my eating plan. Through your grace, remind me that I will reach my goal if I don't give up.[5]

THIRD PRAYERFUL ACTION:
HUMBLY ACKNOWLEDGE TO YOURSELF AND TO GOD,

"I AM POWERLESS ON MY OWN TO CHANGE MY EATING HABITS."

"I just need to find the right diet."

Isn't that the way most of us have thought about weight loss? Publishers love this way of thinking. It lets them publish 10,000 diet books a year.

But who needs another diet? As a chronic dieter, I knew by heart exactly how many calories and what kinds of food make a nutritious eating plan. I just didn't stick to it.

How about saying this instead: "I am a glutton."

Uh-oh. That sounds awful, doesn't it? But it's all about naming.

Theologian J. Raymond Albertson says the right name for overeating *is* gluttony, an old-fashioned word referring to one of the seven deadly sins. Albertson states, "Just as every alcoholic takes the first step toward recovery when he looks squarely in the mirror and admits, 'I am an alcoholic,' we need to take a good look at ourselves and confess, 'I'm a chronic overeater.'" Then we acknowledge that our willpower alone is not enough.

We need a higher power. We need God.

To confess you are powerless is to profess a profound humility, and humility is at the core of all deeply spiritual lives.

In her overeater's blog, Angela P wrote: "When I finally realized I wasn't in control—that this wasn't something I could *ever* do on my own—that was my point of change. People think if you start praying, it gets easy, but it was one of the hardest things I've ever done: throwing myself on God's mercy like that."

A PRAYER OF LETTING GO

> *Oh Lord,*
> *I keep saying "I can do it.*
> *And tomorrow I'll begin."*
> *But without you, I don't do it.*
> *I fall back into the twin sins of*
> *Pride and Gluttony.*
> *Today, I choose to surrender*
> *To your Will.*
> *Help me live and eat*
> *One day at a time.*
> *"Just for today," I can do this.*
> *And humbly I thank you, Oh Lord,*
> *For loving me enough*
> *To help me through it. Amen.*

A FINAL THOUGHT ABOUT GETTING STARTED

How many of us grew up in households where sweets were available and used as pacifiers? You may have heard, "Don't fuss, sweetie. Here, eat a cookie." Or, "Clean your plate. Remember the starving children." Or had moms who made great mashed potatoes but whose idea of fruit and vegetables stopped at canned peaches in heavy syrup and canned green beans. Or who ate a lot of fast-food meals because it was—well, it was faster for our hard-working parents.

We are products of our environments.

As we begin a new way of thinking about food, and a permanent new way of eating, realize that there will be a few slip-ups along the way because we may have learned poor eating habits as very young children.

When a slip occurs, don't throw up your hands and say, "I knew it! I can't do it!"

And give up.

Say to your self, "It's never too late to start my day over."

All we need to do is repent. *Re-think.*

And begin again.

CHAPTER THREE
MAKING CHOICES

"My new goal is to weigh what my driver's license says."

When my children were young, we lived in San Diego. Fifteen years after moving away, my son Andy returned to go to college there. One day he drove to our "old neighborhood" and knocked on the door of a neighbor's house. After warmly greeting Andy, Mrs. Culbertson said, "So, tell me, Andy, does your mother still eat all that ice cream?"

This is what she remembered about me?

At first, I laughed when Andy told the story, and then I fell into one of those critical self-appraisals where all I could do was take myself to task. It's true that for years, ice cream was my number one comfort food. I could eat an entire half-gallon, spooning it right out of the carton, loving the way it softened and melted in my mouth.

"Shame on you for binging on ice cream!" I scolded myself. "What an outlandish impression to leave with someone."

And then, I thought, "But today's a new day. And today I am making new choices."

That is what life is all about.

Choices. Seeing options. Choosing. And if we need to, choosing again.

A Prayer for Choices

> *Oh Lord, in Isaiah it says, "Forget the former things; do not*
> *dwell on the past. See? I am doing a new thing."*
> *Thank you for this reminder.*
> *What I ate and how I thought about food in the past*
> *Does not reflect who I am today.*
> *Today, I choose more wisely.*
> *Today, I commit to a life of eating in moderation.*
> *Strengthen me by your grace to make better choices today.*
> *Amen.*

Jillian Michaels, one of the trainers on NBC's weight loss reality show, *The Biggest Loser*, said in an online interview, "Some people thrive on a strictly high-protein diet, while others do great with fruits, grains and beans. Sometimes it takes trial and error to find the right combination of foods [for you]. As a trainer, I've learned that you also have to take human frailty into account."

So, just as with body shapes, when it comes to shaping our food choices, there is no one-size-fits-all.

What kind of eating program works best for you?

A PRAYER FOR OPTIONS

Almighty God, I pray for your help in
Stepping outside the box I sometimes put myself in.
Help me remember
I never have to feel trapped in my eating behavior.
If something isn't working, I can choose again.
I can choose how I think about myself.
I can choose how I deal with life's ups and downs.
I can choose what works for me in how I eat.
I am not swayed by others' choices.
I am patient with myself.
Help me remember
I can choose.
And if I need to, I can choose again.
And again. Amen.

MANY PEOPLE, MANY CHOICES

Ginny is someone I met through a popular weight loss program that holds weekly meetings and "weigh-ins." She went to the meetings—"religiously" she told me—and, at about two pounds a week, lost eighty-three pounds over the next eleven months. Now that she's reached her goal weight, Ginny still goes once a month to weigh-in so she can "maintain."

Debra, who is single, decided to lose "50 for 50": fifty pounds for her fiftieth birthday and, God bless her, she's kept it off ever since. What works for her is a modified low-carb diet. She eats as much as she wants but only from her list of "allowed" foods. Also, she works for a corporation with an excellent employees' cafeteria, so she eats her main meal there, and keeps very little food at home.

Annie gained thirty-five pounds after she and her husband retired. She opted for a personal trainer at a diet center who gives her a meal plan and expects her to weigh in three times a week. There are no group meetings but plenty of follow-through when she steps on the scale every Monday, Wednesday, and Friday. She admits, "My biggest challenge will be maintaining once I stop meeting with my trainer."

Kelly is a twenty-six year old who found support in cyber-space. She avoided the for-profit web sites, and opted for one that is free and consists of many small groups, each one no larger than four members who check in with each other daily. One woman I know became such "pals" with her online support group that after a year the four of them decided to meet in "real space" at a resort in Florida!

LaKendra had a harder struggle. "I was always the fat kid on the block," she told me. "I learned to make fun of myself before the rest of the kids did, but inside, I was crying. I hated my body." She tried one diet after another, but the weight always came back. At five foot four inches, she weighed 240 pounds.

"I was fat, but I was smart, too, so I created a good career for myself, although, believe me, there's plenty of discrimination against fat people." One of the things LaKendra dreaded most was taking business trips. "When other passengers on a plane watched me walk down the aisle, I knew everyone of them was thinking, 'Please, oh please, don't sit next to me.'"

Last year, at forty years old, she elected to have gastric bypass surgery. "You have to be pretty desperate to do this. But I was beginning to worry about my health. And the surgery has helped." She's lost ninety pounds so far and is continuing to drop.

Lots of choices.

FIRST PRAYERFUL ACTION: MAKE WISE CHOICES IN THE SUPERMARKET

One choice we can make is how we shop for food. Dr. Don Colbert titled his book *What Would Jesus Eat?* The answer, he says, is the food made by God, which medical and health professionals agree is a lot healthier than processed food.

So at your local supermarket, fill your cart with God's food. Circle the store's outside aisles because that's where nature's food is displayed. Start at the fresh veggie and fruit section. Circle around to meats and fish, then to the dairy section for milk, cheese and yogurt. End with cereals and whole grain breads.

Prepared foods, snacks, cookies, and candies are found on

the inside shelves at supermarkets. The more we stay on the perimeter, the better our food choices will be.

A PRAYER OF REAL FOOD

Do you know where your real food comes from?
Do you remember the taste?
Then keep to it and do not meddle with the kind of food
That seems desirable to the other eye,
Feed on the tree of Life and let the pure power
Of God be revealed and manifested in you. Amen.
(Isaac Pennington)

SECOND PRAYERFUL ACTION: CHOOSE PORTION CONTROL

Eating fruits, veggies, whole grains, and lean protein is healthy, but we can still overdo it in portion size. Americans have been "super-sized" for so long, it's hard for us to know what a normal portion is. We must be diligent in retraining ourselves. Here are some ways to do it.

- Buy divided heavy paper plates. Put your salad or vegetable in the biggest of the three spaces, and your meat and complex carbohydrate in the other two.
- Serve yourself on a plate that is smaller than a dinner plate.
- Avoid restaurant buffets.
- Use "eye-balling" reminders of size. A tennis ball

equals a medium apple or pear. Six dice equal
1 ounce of cheese. The palm of your hand equals
4 ounces of meat.

As you serve yourself, or are served, say this short prayer:
I choose right portions
In the name of God who loves me.

A PRAYER OF MANY CHOICES

Oh Lord,
How do I choose?
So many foods arrayed
On supermarket shelves.
Succulent. Delicious.
How do I choose?
At restaurants,
"Hi, I'm your server.
Which salad dressing?"
How do I choose?
In cookie kiosks at the mall.
And colorful ads in magazines
Everywhere I look, there's food.
How do I choose? Wisely?
Your words are my answer, oh Lord.
"I have set before you life and death. . . . Choose life . . .
loving the Lord your God, obeying him, and holding fast
to him." (Deuteronomy 30:19–20)

Touch my mind, God, as I select
What and when and how I eat.
Help me hear your voice when I am tempted.
Infuse me with holy wisdom
In all the ways I choose. Amen.

Chapter Four

Stress Is Not a Synonym for Chocolate

"Stress is when you wake up screaming and realize you haven't fallen asleep yet."

"Want to hear my dirty little secret?" asked Carrie.

"Sure."

"Until I changed the way I ate, my kids never knew that chocolate Easter bunnies had ears."

"No! You didn't—"

"Yes. I did."

We laughed together, but in a rueful way. If she bit off the ears of bunny rabbits, I, for one, once bought a bag of miniature Hershey bars for Halloween handouts, and before the first trick-or-treater arrived, had eaten all but two. Does anything taste better than rich, gooey, melt-in-your-mouth chocolate? Next to ice cream, it was my favorite stress reliever.

CHOCOLATE: A HEALTH FOOD?

Actually, chocolate in moderation *is* beneficial. It contains vitamins A, B1, C, D, and E, plus potassium, sodium, iron, and fluorine. Eating dark chocolate significantly drops blood pressure. Cocoas may help strengthen the immune system.

Of course the key is moderation.

My Aunt Helen has beautiful posture and a body as slim as Nicole Kidman's. She keeps a large brandy snifter filled with Hershey miniatures on her piano. I watched her pick out one of them, *break it in half,* and put the other half back for the next day. I could only marvel at her self-control.

Scripture says, "For the grace of God has appeared, bringing salvation to all, training us to . . . live lives that are self-controlled, upright, and godly" (Titus 2:11–12).

Moderation in all things is also an important part of the spiritual Rule of St. Benedict. "All must be given its due, but *only* its due. There should be something of everything and not too much of anything."

That includes chocolate.

A PRAYER FOR MODERATION

Oh Lord, I pray for a spirit of moderation.
A willingness to say, about what I eat,
Not too much, not too little, But just right.
If I can't moderate my food desires,
How will I overcome larger desires?
Yet I humbly acknowledge
I am weak, Oh Lord,
And when I stress a lot,
Chocolate sings to me.
Strengthen me against the siren's song,
I pray.

STRESS LOVES COMPANY

One evening, I gathered six women friends to talk about how stress influenced their eating. They ranged in age from 29 to 62. "What does stress mean to you?" I began.

As soon as they heard the word, I heard groans and mutters.

Jessica, 30s: "To me, stress means I've run out of time on a project and I'm scrambling."

Megan, 40s: "Everybody wants a piece of me. At work, at home, my husband, my kids and all their sports . . . "

Betty, 60s: "I just retired and feel as if there's too much time to fill. I'm not used to it, so I wander out to the kitchen. . . ."

Stacy, 40s: "I get stressed when I have to make a presentation."

Patty, 50s: "Mortgage payments. We're re-negotiating our loan."

Alli, 29: "My new baby. I love her but no one warned me how hard it can be. I put her down for a nap, and an hour later, she's awake and crying. And I'm sooo tired."

As each woman spoke, the rest of us nodded. We could relate.

Our bodies are great at responding to threats. Muscles tense. Adrenalin increases. Breath comes faster. Heart pounds. Every one of our senses goes on red alert.

But the "fight-or-flight" response is intended for the short-term. A lot of today's stress is chronic and can make us absolutely ravenous for chocolate, pizza, donuts: all things sugary and caloric (not many crave broccoli).

"Still, there must be answers apart from eating. What are your ideas?" I asked my friends.

After laughter and a few, "Hey, that's why I agreed to show up tonight. I'm hoping you'll tell me," the group got more serious.

FROM STRESS TO PEACE

Megan: "I think prayer is a great way to handle stress, but if I'm already opening the refrigerator door, it's too late. So I need to get in the habit of turning to prayer *sooner*."

Jessica: "I'd like to get into the habit of praying more often *during* my day, not just at night or when I wake up. Something simple like, 'Jesus, help me.'"

Stacy: "Deep breathing and repeating on each breath, 'I breathe in all good, I breathe out all fear' helps me when I remember to do it."

Betty: "Maybe if I create a schedule for myself because that's what I used to do at work. It's the lack of structure that's made me eat. Kind of a time-filler, you know? And I think I'll do better if I start my day with prayer *and* with exercise."

Alli: "I thought I had to prove I'm a good mother by doing it all. But the rest of you are encouraging me to get help with the baby. What a relief that would be."

Patty: "I know I eat when I'm worried about money. And I know Scripture says, "Be not afraid," but that hasn't stopped my fear. So maybe I need to keep lots of low-cal snacks on hand, and toss out the high-calorie stuff. Just go with the fear, but in a healthier way."

I summed up, "So, we can turn **Stress** into **Peace** if we

- **P**ractice deep breathing.

- **E**xercise and move.

- **A**cknowledge our eating patterns and substitute healthier foods. Maybe add some structure to our day.

- **C**hoose a simple prayer to use all during the day.

- **E**ntrust others with some of our overload tasks.

Heads nodded. Some of my friends were taking notes.

A Toss-and-Turn Prayer

Okay, God, here's the way I feel right now.
Like the inside of a clothes dryer.
All hot and bothered
With my "stuff."
—Worries and fears and stress, oh my—
Tumbling and tossing around
In my mind until
It makes me dizzy.
When I feel like this, I don't want to pray.
Prayer is just one more stressor.
Who has time or energy
To hallow your name?
(I'm being honest now.)
When I'm stressed,
I wish someone would hallow me.
Help me open the door of this dryer, Oh Lord,

So I can cool down, and then maybe
Pray my gratitude. Amen.

Sometimes, we're reluctant to express ourselves in an honest way to the Creator. As if our innermost thoughts are not already known! The Loving Creator is so much larger than you or I. Our bursts of stressed-out anger never frighten or anger God. God understands us more than we understand ourselves.

Prayer is honest conversation with God and, since we find God's Spirit within our deepest selves, it includes honest self-talk. When we're anxious or worried, a hungry hole opens inside that a lot of us become desperate to fill.

If you can openly acknowledge your feelings and get at their root cause, you'll be more likely to cope with stress *without* filling the hole with food.

> Between *stimulus* and *response* there is a
> space,
> And in that space is our power to choose a
> response.
> And in what we choose lies growth and
> freedom.[6]

First Prayerful Action: Repetitive Prayer

Repetitive prayer can be very calming when you're stressed.

In recent years, I've trained myself to repeat the name of Jesus when I am driving or walking or taking dishes from the dishwasher—any action that doesn't demand complete attention. I fall easily into mentally repeating "Jesus, Jesus, Jesus" or "Jesus, mercy. Christ, have mercy."

The words act like a gentle underground river, flowing beneath my other thoughts. I feel as if Jesus helps me through stressful times when I remember to say his name.

An alternative is to tell yourself you won't eat until you have "counted to ten with God." Then say, "One-for God, two-for-God, three-for-God, and so on."

End with, "All for God." Immediately drink eight ounces of water, both as a way to fill yourself and because water is a powerful spiritual symbol.

Do you still want to eat? Often, the answer is no.

Another alternative is a one-minute time-out or 60-second fast.

- Drink a big glass of water.
- Breathe slowly, deeply.
- Offer the minute to God, saying,

  Between my thoughts and my actions, Oh Lord,
  I place your Presence. Amen.[7]

Chances are, at the end of a minute, you'll be able to face down your temptation.

And if you do give in? Well, remember, God forgives you. Forgive yourself.

SECOND PRAYERFUL ACTION:
MAP THE PATTERN OF YOUR STRESSORS

It's not always a big stressor that gets to us. It may be the accumulation of daily hassles and demands. Over time persistent little things can accumulate and wreak more havoc than a sudden big thing.

One way to map the pattern of your stress is to keep a stress journal for one week.

- Note exactly which events and situations cause a negative physical, mental or emotional response.

- Record the day and time. Briefly describe the situation.

- Where were you?

- Who was involved?

- What seemed to cause the stress?

- What was your reaction? Did you have any physical symptoms? What did you say or do?

- Was food involved? How and what?

- Finally, on a scale of 1 (not very intense) to 5 (very intense), rate the intensity of your stress.

Look closely at the events that you ranked as *very* stressful. Select just one to work on in the coming week.

A STRESS PRAYER

Infinite Creator,
When life feels out of control,
Fill my inner space with grace
So I will not fill it with food.
In Christ's name, I pray.

THIRD PRAYERFUL ACTION:
TAKE SOMETHING OFF YOUR "PLATE"

Ever noticed that when we have too much to do, we say, "I have too much on my plate"? Sometimes it becomes literally true. We put too much food on our plates.

"I've been trying to eat wisely," said Sarah, "but this week, our kitchen was all torn up because we're remodeling. My husband was irritated and acting unpleasant. And I had problems at work. Suddenly I found myself almost *inhaling* two cold hot dogs and a bunch of potato chips. Definitely not on my eating plan. And as soon as I ate a few chips, I wanted more. Even though I was eating so fast, I hardly tasted them."

When we're racing the clock, we often eat unconsciously, stuffing food into our mouths because we think we don't have time to slow down.

That's precisely the time to

- **Stop.** Simply stop whatever you're doing.
- Take a deep, slow breath, and then

Say aloud from the Psalm, *"Be still and know I am God."*

- Take another deep breath, and say, *"Be still and know I am."*
- Another slow breath. *"Be still and know."*
- *"Be still."*
- *"Be."*
- *"Be."* Between each repetition of the word, breathe slowly.
- *"Be."*

Remind yourself, "If I take a few things off my things-to-do plate, I will be less inclined to put too much on my food plate."

Fourth Prayerful Action: Just Say No!

Many times life feels out of balance because we are over-committed. Here is a three-step process to help you say "No."

1. *Listen to the request* all the way through without interrupting. Say this quick prayer to yourself: *I am strengthened in the Lord.*
2. *Say "No" immediately.* Do not equivocate. For example, "I am honored you asked, but I can't join the committee because of the demands of my job and family at this time."

3. *Offer an alternative* in some situations. For instance, "I can't work late tonight because of my son's birthday party, but I could come in an hour early tomorrow."

From a spiritual perspective, admitting to yourself and another that you can't "do it all" is a way of fostering humility, which is the basis of a prayerful relationship with God. Remember, even competent people drop balls they're juggling when they have too much to do.

And they may overeat.

CHAPTER FIVE
GRACE BEFORE AND AFTER MEALS
(AND EVEN IN BETWEEN)

"Blessed are those who hunger and thirst, for they are sticking to their diets."

When I was growing up, my family prayed before dinner, "Bless us, Oh Lord, for these, thy gifts, which we are about to receive through thy bounty." We didn't say grace before other meals, though. My stepson and his family say grace before every meal, even when they're eating out. Theirs is a very simple prayer:

*"God is great, God is good. Let us thank him
for our food."*

I like the idea of inviting God to be with us as we begin
our meals. Nutritionists say that the best eating plans are built
around regular meals—either the traditional three, or five
smaller meals. So we have at least three opportunities each and
every day to call on God's grace to aid us in moderate eating.

Breakfast, the meal that breaks our night's fast, is the most
important meal of the day. A Stanford University study found
that people who ate breakfast not only were more successful in
losing weight, they were also more successful in keeping it off.

Here's a delightful little prayer I came across online: *"For
bacon, eggs and buttered toast, praise Father, Son and Holy
Ghost."*

After a good breakfast,

- You are likely to eat less at lunch and dinner.
- You'll have better mid- to late-morning concentration.
- You'll improve your ability to solve problems.
- Calories consumed early in the day are used primarily
  for fuel vs. nighttime calories that tend to be stored
  as fat.

And at least two long-term university studies claim that
people who eat breakfasts live longer!

A DIETER'S BREAKFAST PRAYER

(You might copy this prayer and tape it to your refrigerator where it will be easy to see and say.)

Today, I fill my body
With God's good food.
And commit to right eating
Throughout the day.
I will praise God
In the food I eat,
The thoughts I think,
The actions I take.
In the name of the
Creator, the Redeemer, and the Sanctifier, Amen.

BLESSING BEFORE A MID-MORNING SNACK

I give thanks to God
For apples and pears,
For baby carrots
And celery sticks.
I give thanks for hot tea
And my bottle of water;
For no-cal soda
And whatever else keeps me away
From vending machine temptation.

For all healthy snacks
And the commitment I've made

To eat in a new and better way,
I give thanks and praise God!

One way to make sure healthy snacks are available is to take them to work with you. As you pack a small thermal container, ask God to bless this food and your "right use" of it.

FIRST PRAYERFUL ACTION: DRINK MORE WATER

- Sometimes hunger is not hunger at all, but thirst.
- Nutritionists recommend drinking six glasses of water a day.
- Drinking twelve ounces of water a half hour before eating will help you eat less.
- Spiritually, water is a powerful symbol. References abound in Scripture.
- Every time you drink water, give thanks for a blessing you have received.

Thank you, Lord, for watering my soul
With this blessing (name your blessing).
May I never take any of my blessings for granted. Amen.

ANOTHER WATER PRAYER

I thank the earth for feeding my body,
I thank the sun for warming my bones,
I thank the trees for the air I breathe,
And I thank this water for nourishing my soul.[8]

SECOND PRAYERFUL ACTION: AVOID MULTITASKING MEALS

"When I was little," said Amanda, "I liked to read the backs of cereal boxes while I ate breakfast. Then I started reading comic books while I ate. Later, it was the newspaper. Eating and reading are very connected for me."

I completely understood. Any time I eat alone, I pick up something to read. I've been doing it so long that in my mind, the two actions are intimately intertwined. And if I want to keep reading, my excuse becomes, "I'm still eating," which means I go looking for more food!

Jim likes to eat and do the daily crossword puzzle, and if he's having a hard time working it, he, too, keeps munching.

Shanta frequently eats lunch at her desk, chewing fast while she punches her computer keyboard. Linda, who lives alone, often eats dinner in front of her TV. "I'll finish dinner and move to a bag of chips. *American Idol* just isn't the same without my bag of chips."

Multitasking can throw off anyone's ideal eating program.

These days, it's commonplace to look for "two-fers." We think we get more done when we do two things at once, even though research shows that multitasking actually makes us *less* productive.

It's not a good idea to multitask meals. Make it your goal to do just one thing when you eat:

Eat.

THIRD PRAYERFUL ACTION: EAT MINDFULLY

Eating mindfully goes beyond simply eating. Instead of bolting food, the idea is to eat slowly and deliberately, experiencing the texture, aroma and delicious natural taste of food.

Sarah described a beautiful October day when she was hiking with a friend in the mountains. "We ate lunch beside a stream in a high mountain meadow. I had packed a peanut butter sandwich and an apple. Oh, the crunch of that apple! The chewiness of the multigrain bread! I was so *aware* of the flavors. So aware of the rippling water, the feel of long grass against my fingers, the clouds moving fast across the blue sky."

Sarah was experiencing mindfulness. She was *in* the moment.

So often, we're either thinking about the past or planning or worrying about the future. Either way, we're not alive to the moment. Mindfulness lets us notice what is happening—right now! We observe how we are responding mentally, emotionally and physically to our situation.

By freeing us from unconscious eating, it can help us improve how we eat.

START SMALL

- Carefully select *four* bites of food.
- Inhale the aroma of each bite. Really look at the color, shape, and visual texture of an orange slice. A garden-ripe tomato. Fresh green beans.

- Try and shut out other stimuli while you chew.
- Concentrate on each bite's taste and texture. Notice your act of swallowing. As much as possible, engage all five senses.

A Mindfulness Prayer before Eating

I open my heart and my senses to this moment,
To this single bite of food.
To this act of partaking of a gift from mother earth.
I am aware. I give thanks.
I take nothing for granted.

Fourth Prayerful Action: Dine Out Sensibly

"When I started practicing my new way of eating, it was very hard at first to go to a restaurant with friends," said Kim. "The waiter would plop a basket of bread on the table, and I couldn't send it back because my friends wanted some. Then I'd be tempted to eat a piece, especially if service was slow and our main meal hadn't come.

"You know how big restaurant portions are. For a long time, a little part of me would whisper, 'Go ahead and eat it. After all, you're paying for it.' Finally, I began asking *immediately* for a 'doggie bag' and I'd put half my portion in it as soon as I was served. That helped. I also liked to order grilled fish and get double veggies instead of potatoes or rice.

"Whenever I made it through a restaurant meal sensibly, I always said a small prayer of thanks as I paid my check."

Dear Lord,
Thank you for the pleasure of eating with friends.
Thank you for the strength to eat wisely and well.

A PRAYER AFTER AN ENTIRE DAY OF "RIGHT EATING"

Halleluiah! I did it!
Today has been a day of right eating.
And making good choices.
Not all were easy. I was tempted,
Yet today, I chose well.
"My grace is sufficient for you,
for power is made perfect in weakness. (2 Corinthians 12:9)
Thank you for working in me, Lord.
Through your power, I was strengthened in my weakness.
Alleluia! Alleluia!

CHAPTER SIX
LEAD US NOT INTO TEMPTATION

"When you're dieting, won't power is better than will power."

Here's something I read on a dieter's online message board: "Every day, I see it! The great big bowl of candy Susan keeps on her receptionist's desk. I used to grab a piece or two every time I walked by, without even thinking about it. Now I try and resist, but it's very hard."

Yes, temptations don't go away when we commit to new eating habits. Sometimes they seem to get bigger.

When you're tempted, consider these words from *The Imitation of Christ*: "The *source* of temptation is in *ourselves*. When one temptation passes, another is on its way. We cannot win this battle by running away. Meet temptations at the door as soon as they knock and do not let them in. Little by little, through patience and endurance of spirit, And with the help of God, you *will* win a victory."⁹

A QUICK PRAYER WHILE TURNING AWAY A TEMPTATION

Temptation is knocking.
With God's help, I shut the door.

FIRST PRAYERFUL ACTION: COMMIT TO "LITTLE BY LITTLE"

A few years ago, I saw an article titled, "I lost 300 pounds." *Wow*, I thought. But the opening line set me straight: "That's because I lost the same 30 pounds ten times."

Starting a hot "new diet" is always tempting. Maybe, we think, this will be "the one." But experts say *any* diet works in the short term because diets, by definition, are restrictive, and restricting our calories takes off weight.

Short-term.

But our goal is to reach a healthy weight (not skinny, just healthy) and then maintain it. The best long-term weight loss occurs slowly, at about two pounds a week. If your goal is losing fifty pounds, that means six months. (If your immediate response is, "Oh no! I want to do it faster!" you're still thinking about short-term diets instead of a permanent change in eating habits.)

Avoid the temptation to sweep away everything you're used to eating: Out, potatoes! Out, fast food! Out, chocolate! Out, red meat!

Focus on *improving* your diet in important little ways.

Replace snacks and fast foods with fruits and veggies. Eat toast with apple butter instead of real butter. Poach an egg instead of frying it. Mix tuna and lettuce instead of tuna and mayonnaise. There are many books and many online resources that can help.

Don't think about fifty pounds or six months. Focus on
• Just one meal.
• Just one day.
• Just one week.

Pray before meals, and concentrate on working with God to eat wisely. Little by little, habits will change. Pounds will come off. And this time, they'll stay off.

It's the same with prayer. When I started practicing meditative prayer—sitting in silence with God every day—nothing seemed to happen at first. My thoughts were scattered. I didn't feel bathed in holiness. I was tempted to quit. Then I read these words: "When a dragonfly sits, it simply sits, not focused on future flights, past adventures, or an encounter with another dragonfly.

Meditation is what sitting is to a dragonfly"[10]

Don't get antsy about your weight loss. Be a dragonfly.

"JUST THIS ONCE"

When Keli was invited to join friends for a football tailgate party, she gulped. She wanted to go, but she knew what the food would be: Nachos and cheese dip. Hot dogs and chili. Beer. Everything she had sworn off eating two months earlier.

"Oh come on," said her friend Shamil. "Don't be a stick in the mud! Give up your diet just this once."

As she spoke to me later, Keli told me her choices were

- Listen to Shamil and eat tailgate fare, but keep it in small portions. ("The problem is, I know myself. Once I started, it would be hard to eat 'just a little.'")

- Turn down the party. ("But I don't want to deprive myself of friends and fun just because I'm trying to make wiser choices when I eat.")

- Plan an alternative, which might include taking her own food.

Keli chose the third option and packed a lunch that included fruit and yogurt. She also ate a large salad at home right before she left. Most of the people at the party didn't even realize she was eating something different.

SECOND PRAYERFUL ACTION: BE ALERT FOR SABOTEURS

"Just this once" is one of the most devious of tempting phrases. It's a favorite with secret saboteurs—those friends and loved ones who also say,

- "Why are you dieting? You look fine."
- "You don't need to lose weight."
- "But I made this dessert just for you."

Arm yourself against sabotage by creating responses in advance.

To someone who says you don't need to lose weight:

"Thanks, but I'm changing my eating habits for health reasons, not just to lose weight."

To someone who offers you unwanted food:

- "No, thank you." (Said nicely but firmly.)
- "Thanks, but I just ate."
- "I appreciate your making these for me. I'll take them home." (Then, straight to the garbage disposal.)

When tempted to sabotage yourself, say this line out loud:

"*Nothing* tastes as good as being thin feels."

A PRAYER OF RESISTANCE

Oh Lord, I am so tempted.
Should I give in "just this once"?
Siren voices are calling.
But if I give in now,
Won't it be harder to resist the next time?
I turn to Jesus for help.
You were tempted in the desert
And three times said no.
Strengthen my resistance, so that
Just this once, I, too,
Can say no.

THIRD PRAYERFUL ACTION:
IDENTIFY TEMPTING SITUATIONS AND ENVIRONMENTS

I have mentioned this before, but it bears repeating.

"Nighttime is the worst," says Sarah. "I stick to my diet during the day, but at night—especially cold winter nights— I crave chips 'n popcorn."

She's not alone. Eighty percent of dieters say evenings are their hardest times. And if you wake up in the middle of the night—well, everyone's heard of this law: "Food eaten in the middle of the night has no calories." Right?

Another friend says about her nighttime eating: "It's a balanced diet: I balance dark chocolate with white chocolate."

When I traveled a lot on business, my big temptation came at airports. Whenever my flight was delayed, I'd feel sorry for myself and head straight for the ice cream stand. "Poor me, stuck in this airport. I *deserve* to eat a triple-decker cone."

A PRAYER OF SUPPLICATION

> *Oh Lord, come to my aid in this moment of need.*
> *Save me from self-sabotage*
> *When I tell myself, "I deserve to eat this because . . . "*
> *(Because my spouse hurt my feelings,*
> *Because I got turned down for a promotion,*
> *Because my flight got cancelled,*
> *Because no one realizes just how much I do . . .).*
> *Help me claim what your apostle Paul promised.*
> *"God will not let you be tempted*
> *Beyond what you can bear . . .*
> *He will provide a way out*
> *So you can stand up under it."*
>
> *I remember*
> *What another of your disciples wrote:*
> *"The pleasure of giving into temptation is like smoke . . .*
> *It vanishes quickly.*
> *Soon even the memory of joy is gone."*[11]

WHEN A CRAVING FOR NIGHTTIME MUNCHIES HITS

Force yourself to get up off the sofa, even if it means missing your favorite TV show. On your radio or iPod, play some fast music and do something *active*.

- Lift weights, do stretches, march in place, or dance.
- Clean one of your dresser drawers or a closet shelf.
- Sweep and mop the kitchen floor.
- Phone a friend, perhaps an out of town friend you haven't talked to in awhile.

Recall these words from Romans 12:2: "Be transformed by the renewing of your minds, so that you may discern what is the will of God."

Oh Lord, transform my desire for food into holy action, I pray.

WHEN YOU FEEL DISCOURAGED

All week, I tried to be so good in the way I ate. Yet when I stepped on the scale this morning, I'd gained a pound! How can that be? I'm so discouraged! So tempted to just give up. In times past, I might have walked right out to the kitchen and fixed myself French toast, oozing with butter and warm syrup.

But today I am taking time to pray, and I discovered these words, by Teresa of Avila: "It is the Lord's will that we should be tested. . . . If then, you sometimes fall, do not lose heart. Even more, do not cease striving to make progress. Be resolute."

I will not give in and eat something fattening.
If I stick to good eating habits,
I will see results.
If not today, then tomorrow.
God, strengthen me to stay resolute.
Tomorrow, who knows what the scale will show?

FAST FOOD VS. FASTING

My friend Janie said, "You know how I clean up my dining room? I pick up the fast food wrappers off the floor of my car."

I laughed, but it is true. We are a "fast-food society."

Look at some calorie counts I gleaned from the Internet:

• Double Whopper® with Cheese: 990 calories

• Cheese fries: 3,110 calories.

• Egg McMuffin™ and hash browns: 900 calories

Whew! Eat one fast-food breakfast, and you've consumed three-fourths of your calories for the day.

Instead of eating fast food, maybe we should think more about fasting, which incorporates mindfulness. In Scripture, people of the Bible fasted for many reasons:

• For deliverance (2 Chronicles 20:3)

• To mourn the loss of a loved one (1 Samuel 31:13)

- For healing (Psalm 35:13)

- For spiritual strength (Matthew 4:2)

- To increase willpower and self-discipline (1 Corinthians 9:27)

Moses fasted for forty days and nights, and so did Jesus in the desert.

What Is a Fast?

A fast is *not* the same as a diet. Nor is it intended merely to jump-start our diets. A fast is a spiritual tool that can bring us closer to God and help us know ourselves better. The more we know ourselves and our inner motivations, the more likely we are to understand our unhealthy eating habits. Then we can look for substitute behaviors.

For whatever period of time—whether ten minutes, half a day, twenty-four hours, or even, under special circumstances such as a guided retreat, for several days—fasting means abstaining from food for a spiritual purpose.

Author Richard Foster says, "Physical benefits . . . must never replace God as the center of our fasting." But by fasting as a way to honor God, we will discover, once we take away food, some of the things that control us. "Anger, bitterness, jealousy, strife, fear . . . if they are within us, they will surface during fasting," says Foster.

A BEGINNER'S FAST

If you have never fasted before, a manageable fast is one that goes from one lunch time to the next, so you skip two meals: dinner and breakfast. Although you abstain from food, be sure to drink plenty of water and other clear liquids. Outwardly, your day will continue as usual, but inwardly, every slight twinge of hunger will remind you to give thanks and praise God.

In the prophet Isaiah's time, people grumbled that they had fasted, yet God did not answer in the way they wanted (Isaiah 58:3–4). Isaiah responded by proclaiming that the external show of fasting and prayer, without the proper *heart attitude*, was futile (Isaiah 58:5–9). Inner motivation is the key.

Jesus instructed: "When you fast, . . . [do it] so that your fasting may be seen not by others but by your Father who is in secret; and your Father who sees in secret will reward you" (Matthew 6:17–18).

CHAPTER SEVEN
DIETERS NEED FRIENDS, TOO

"Just when you think you've reached bottom, someone tosses you a shovel."

Regardless of how handsome the body, its beauty is lifeless unless the soul is bubbling up out of it. To create a fountain of living water requires daily digging deeper into your inner well of spirit. Prayer is the shovel. Use it.[12]

Church pastor Kevin Jones lost 140 pounds with the aid

of prayer, diet, exercise, *and*, he says fondly, the encouragement of his wife, Irene. He applauds Irene for never criticizing him while he was fat, and for doing everything she could to help him once he committed to lose weight. "She'd even hold down my feet while I did sit-ups," he says.

Research shows conclusively that dieters who have support systems show less stress, are more likely to reach their goals and—here comes the important part—*are better able to maintain their successes.*

We humans are sociable creatures. We like to feel a part of a family, a group, a tribe. It is true that a Harvard University study found obesity can be "contagious" through social networks; that is, if a close friend gains a lot of weight, your chances of gaining weight increase by an amazing 71 percent. Apparently, it stretches your own idea of acceptable body size.

Still, companionship generally is a plus in life.

One of my favorite true stories is about a man I'll call Bob. After doctors told him his cancer was terminal, he e-mailed every one he knew and said, "The docs are telling me I'll soon be extinct. But that's what people thought about buffalo, and they made a comeback. Will you join my buffalo herd?" He asked members of his "herd" to regularly send him funny stories and upbeat, motivational encouragement.

Bob lived six *years* longer than doctors predicted. And his story inspired others to start their own "buffalo herds."

A business colleague in my city wanted to change careers. He formed a "sabbatical committee" of six friends and business mentors who agreed to meet with him once a month for six months. They offered feedback as he talked through the pros and cons of various career possibilities.

The speaker at my son's college graduation said, "The more people I know, the luckier I get." People can help us when we're losing weight, and at other times, too.

A Prayer of Association

> Oh Lord, Give me wisdom to
> Heed the wise words
> Of Theresa of Avila:
> "Associate with others who
> are walking in the right way;
> Not only those who are
> where we are in the journey
> but also those who have gone farther."

Our support may come from
- Local Friends
- Family Friends
- Spiritual Friends
- Fitness Friends
- Online Friends
- God as Friend.

You might know a person in every one of those groups. Or you may find all the support you need in just one or two.

A PRAYER FOR "RIGHT SUPPORT"

Oh God, my Divine Friend,
Jesus knew our need for fellowship.
He said, "Where two or more are gathered in my name."
Bring into my life the right
People, books, web sites;
Whatever support I need
To permanently change
How I eat and live.
I can't do it alone.
In confidence I turn to you.
My Beloved Friend.

FIRST PRAYERFUL ACTION: ASK THIS QUESTION

"What qualities do I need in my supporters?" Write down your answers. Spend a little time with this.

Think about the people you know. The closest family member may—or may not—be your best support as you change eating habits. A close family member may fear that if you change, it will threaten your relationship. And the truth is it will require changes as you stock the pantry with low-calorie foods and make time for exercise. Most of all, your confidence will shoot up as you take control of your eating. In some marital relationships, that can be the most threatening of all.

Here's my list of what it takes to be a good supporter, formed by my own experience, from talking to others, and from going online.

What Great Supporters DO

- They help you strategize a good eating plan—but only if invited to do so.

- They offer encouragement, especially if you should momentarily fall.

- If you live in the same home, they keep wholesome foods on hand.

- They share their own stories and their own struggles.

- They have a good sense of humor and keep life upbeat.

- Some may change their own eating habits to keep you company.

- When hosting a party, they consider your need for low-calorie food.

- They look for ways to get together that are non-food based.

Margot and her husband began to walk right after work. Before, they would catch up with each other over wine and cheese and crackers. "Walking two miles is a lot better," she says.

Two women I know meet regularly for pedicures. "We treat our feet and catch up on conversation," says Ashley. "We love it! And pedicures have no calories."

What Great Supporters DON'T DO

- They never criticize or make fun of you.

- They don't act like "Food Police" and tell you what to do.

- They don't announce to the world that you're on a diet.

- They don't use secret sabotage by bringing home the "danger foods" you love or by pressing you to eat something you have taken off your food list.

A BLESSING PRAYER FOR A WEIGHT-LOSS COMPANION

Thank you, oh Lord, for _____.
I ask you to meet her (or his) needs this day.
Bless our time together.
May we honor You
As well as help each other. Amen.

A PRAYER OF FORGIVENESS FOR A FALTERING FRIEND

Oh Holy Healer, I feel let down by (fill in the
*   name) _____.*
I counted on her (his) support.
Instead, I heard hurtful words.
Now the words I want her (him) to say,
The words "I'm sorry"
Are covered up with
"I was only kidding. Where's your sense of humor?"
Laughing off the hurt
Is more than I can do,

But through your loving grace
May I find in my heart
Willingness to just let it go.
In the name of Jesus Christ,
The great forgiver. Amen.

EXERCISE BUDDIES

Having an exercise buddy is a particularly great way to notch up your commitment to your new way of life because the two of you may be able to combine fitness *and* good eating.

For more than a year, Anne and I met at a park three times a week to walk. More times than I can count, especially in colder months, I was tempted to roll over for added snooze time, except . . . "Annie's waiting. I'd better get up."

A special gift in our walks was our shared commitment to a deeper spiritual life. Sure, we talked about ordinary "stuff": husbands, kids, jobs, and, yes, food. We also talked about our relationship with God and how to live Christian values in our everyday lives.

SPIRITUAL FRIENDS

Many churches have started weight-loss support groups. Weigh-Down and First Place are two of the best known and hold meetings in more than 10,000 churches around the country. Their programs incorporate Scripture and prayer.

Overeaters Anonymous, like all twelve-step programs, has always had a spiritual, though not religious, component.

Participants acknowledge with the very first step, "I am power-less over my addiction" and they turn to a Higher Power.

T.O.P.S. (Take Off Pounds Sensibly), though it doesn't talk about any specific church doctrine, holds many of its local meetings in churches.

Second Prayerful Action: Go Online

Finding diet companions online is surely one of the great-est innovations in weight-loss management since the invention of no-cal sweetener. When I googled "Weight Loss Support Groups," an astounding twelve million hits popped up.

The challenge is in finding the right group for you. It may take some experimentation and checking out—even joining— different sites. Most web sites are free, and I list several on the resource page of this book. Some, such as Weight Watchers or Jenny Craig, have a fee. I make no personal recommendations, although I have visited all those I name.

On the web you can find everything you need to help your eating program:

nutrition advice, menus, recipes, specific exercises you can do at home, encouragement from others, live broadcasts. If anything, the sheer quantity can be overwhelming. It's a little like a delicious smorgasbord where you're trying to decide what to put on your plate.

A Prayer before Going Online

Beloved God, you who said
"I will instruct you and teach you
the way you should go" (Psalm 32:8)
Guide me as I surf the web.
Help me use good common sense
As I view the vast array of choices.
It feels good to know
I am not alone;
That others seek to
Control their eating.
But which online program is best for me?
Humbly I pray to be led
By your Spirit. Amen.

God as Friend

What air is to the body, prayer is to the soul, which is why the Master told us to pray unceasingly. Prayer is communion and contact with the Source of Life.[13]

CHAPTER SEVEN
GET MOVING! SWEAT YOUR PRAYER

"Every time I hear the word exercise, I wash my mouth out with chocolate."

When you think about exercising, do you have Annie's problem? She's a forty-something mom who juggles a job, a family and carpooling her kids to their various sporting events. She says, "The only part of my body that gets exercised is my foot pushing the gas pedal."

Ginny used to walk her dog, but lately she's been working such long hours, she had to hire a dog walker.

Emma was embarrassed to go to a fitness center and see "all those svelte bodies. I'm fat and out of shape and I could feel them staring at me."

Teena just plain doesn't like to exercise. "I guess it's not politically correct to say this, but I think exercise is *boring*," she told me.

There are lots of reasons why people don't exercise.

But exercise is key to increasing metabolism and burning off excess fat, so we have to include it in our weight-loss program. Thirty minutes a day will do it, and the good news is, breaking the half hour into three ten-minute intervals works too.

Plus, it makes us feel good. Medical researchers disagree about why. Is it a release of endorphins, the neurotransmitters in the brain that reduce pain and bring euphoria? Or does the good feeling come simply from meeting a physical challenge? Whatever the cause, exercise definitely helps discharge depression and increases a person's sense of well-being. I exercise for my mind as well as my body.

Still, I know a lot of people share Teena's viewpoint.

Do you find excuses for not exercising?

- "I'm too tired!"
- "I'll be late for work!"
- "It's dark outside."
- "It's too cold."

- "I need to run errands."
- "I can't afford the fitness center dues."

A COUCH POTATO'S PRAYER

Oh Lord, listen to my excuses.
I say each one so plausibly.
But you call on us to use our gifts.
And our bodies are one of your greatest gifts.
"In the image of God he created them." (Genesis 1:27)
So incredibly made. Such precision. Such beauty.
Why would I let God's gift grow stiff with disuse?
Why would I let my muscles become lax, and my bones
     weaken?
Why would I fail to strengthen my heart and lungs and
     cardiovascular system?
"Present your bodies as a living sacrifice, holy and
acceptable to God, which is your spiritual worship."
     (Romans 12:1)
No more excuses, Lord.
Your will, not my will be done.
Humbly I do pray.
Help this couch potato
To get up, get out, and get moving!

Despite her fear of people's stares, Emma, who admitted she was fat, did join a gym. This is what she wrote, "The beginning was very hard. I could not run for more than 30 seconds, so I started out walking. Slowly I added weights. I kept reminding myself that I wasn't in competition with anyone else. I just wanted to improve myself.

"Gradually, I saw my body transform. After six months I could lift heavy weights and jog for ten minutes, and I'd lost 40 pounds. A year later, I had reached my goal weight, and now I exercise five times a week. My confidence and self-esteem are up like never before."

TALK BACK PRAYER

If you feel afraid or embarrassed, talk back to the inner voice in your head that tries to hold you back from exercising.

"What if I hurt myself?" *"I'll take proper precautions."*

"What if I fail?" *"I'll try again."*

"What if people stare at me?" *"I'll smile and ask for their support."*

"It's too hard." *"Not if I break it into smaller steps."*

Listen for any negative thinking. Say to yourself, "I *can* do this" and then add what the apostle Paul said: *"Not I, but the Christ in me."*

FIRST PRAYERFUL ACTION: FIND THE RIGHT EXERCISE FOR YOU

A treadmill in her den works for my cousin, a busy lawyer. Eileen gets on her treadmill first thing in the morning, prays the rosary as she walks, then heads for the shower.

Elizabeth likes water aerobics.

Cathy enjoys an hour of solitude in the pool. She gets to her fitness center at 5:45 a.m. Usually, no one else is there. While she alternately walks in the water and swims, she prays. "I suppose you could call it a two-fer," she said. "I exercise my soul and my body at the same time."

Experiment. Try different kinds of exercise. See which one turns you on.

WALKING, WALKING, WALKING

It's the simplest of all. And it's free. Just step outside your front door and begin.

A brisk twenty– or thirty-minute walk can have the same calming effect as a mild tranquilizer. When slower walkers add deep breathing, their sense of well-being equals that of faster walkers.

Even more powerful results occur if you combine walking with a repetitive prayer, such as "God is love," or "The Lord is my shepherd."

Bonnie gets up early in the morning to walk in the woods behind her house. "The first thing I feel is a loosening in my shoulders, as if a weight has lifted," she says. "My breathing rhythm changes. I look out for roots, but I look up, too, because I love to spot birds. Next to our property is a waterfall near an old stone bridge that was built in the 1930s. As I walk, I listen to the splashing water and the noises of woodland creatures, and the twitter of birds, and I feel as if my *soul* is touched by God." Bonnie says her prayer is always, *"Show me the direction you want me to go, oh Lord. Show me the way for today."*

Five days a week, Carol walks three miles to a nearby cemetery. Her grandparents are buried there and it's a very peaceful place. She says, "Reading tombstones reminds me that life is a gift, and all of us eventually give the gift back to God. It helps keep me centered on what's really important."

DANCING YOUR PRAYER

Have you ever been home alone, put on a music CD, and then blissfully danced around your living room—bending, twirling, twisting, swaying,—expressing yourself in a way you never would if you thought someone was watching?

"Dance increases the experience of the Divine, and in many traditions has been as much a part of religious expression as music," wrote Janet Weeks in *Dance* magazine.[14]

What a wonderful way to pray! Loosening our bodies, moving our feet, and experiencing the oneness—the harmony—that comes from praising the Lord with the rhythm of dance. *"Sing to the Lord a new song . . . .Praise his name with dancing, making melody to him with tambourine and lyre"* (Psalm 149:1, 3).

IS BICYCLING FOR YOU?

You've heard people say, "It's like riding a bicycle. It comes back to you."

When I was nine, I owned a girl's blue Schwinn with a white wicker basket. It was forty years before I climbed onto my next bicycle, a skinny-tired, second-hand road bike.

And it did come back! I loved the feel of the wheels turning, and the new way I saw city and countryside. Bicycling became, for me, an act of meditation in motion. And it reminded me of some of life's important truths:

- *When headed into a headwind, accept it.*

  Embrace it. It makes you stronger. I picture "The Little Engine that Could," except I say, "With God I can, With God I can."

- *On a steep hill, don't look all the way up.*

  If you do, the final goal may seem out of reach. On hills, I pay attention only to the yellow line on my immediate left. The top of the hill will come in its own good time.

  Reaching a weight-loss goal will also come in good time if you stay faithful to your program.

  Prepare yourself.

  Shift gears *before* the hill. Drink water *before* you're thirsty. It's the same with eating.

- Eat the right food *before* you get terribly hungry. Think about how you will eat *before* you attend the party.

DIGGING IN THE DIRT

My daughter-in-law's favorite exercise is gardening. When Tami looked it up online, she learned that gardening burns as many calories as a brisk walk. More importantly, she says gardening feeds her soul. Kneeling in the soil is like a natural stance for prayer. "And when my daffodils come up each spring, it's like God reminding me of the Resurrection."

A PLANTING PRAYER

Praise God for the joy I feel
In planting, seeding, watering, weeding.
For the nurturing of nature in all seasons.
Today, Lord, plant in me the seed of Love.
Let it grow as green shoots grow in spring soil
And blossom with everyone I meet.

WHEN LIFE INTERFERES

Okay, but with the best intentions in the world, other priorities occasionally throw off our exercise schedule. Once that happens—once the habit is interrupted—it can seem harder and harder to re-start.

A PRAYER FOR AN EXERCISE DROPOUT

Oh Lord, I reflect on the words of Isaiah,
"Those who wait for the Lord
Shall renew your strength,
They shall mount up with wings like eagles,
They shall run and not be weary,

They shall walk and not faint" (Isaiah 40:31).

For too long, oh Lord, I have not
Walked, run or exercised enough,
Always having a perfectly good reason
Why my day is too full to include one more thing.
Today, I affirm, through your love for me,
A renewed spirit that resolves to start again.
If I cannot immediately soar with eagles' wings,
Let me at least march
With a penguin's steadfastness. Amen.

CHAPTER NINE
MORE EXCERCISES FOR SOUL AND BODY

"When it comes to exercising, my leotards run faster than I do."

Some wag said, "Life is short. Running makes it seem longer." I agree with the first part. Life *is* short. And no one is guaranteed a particular life span. But the more we practice good habits of eating and exercise, the more we can improve our lives—and hopefully lengthen our years.

Here are ten more ways to integrate your body and spirit.

1. CREATE YOUR INTENTION

Spiritual masters say that any activity done with "right motive" engages our best energy. So before you begin exercising, affirm your intent to combine the physical and spiritual.

Two affirmations I like are these:

- *"Let my spirit move in prayerful concert with my body."*
- *"I invite God to be with me as I exercise today."*

2. BREATHE

Breathe deeply and consciously before exercising. As you inhale, picture that you are drawing in God's Holy Spirit. As you exhale, picture yourself releasing any negative toxins of anxiety, fear and impatience. Keep breathing evenly *during* your exercise.

My breath prayer: *"I breathe in all good. I release all bad."*

3. STRETCH

Stretching keeps us limber and flexible—important as we grow older. As you stretch your legs, arms, neck, shoulders, and back, invite your soul to open as well.

Keep me flexible, oh Lord.
Stretch my mind as I stretch my body.
Help me greet the unexpected in life
With a willing spirit, and
A cheerful heart. Amen.

4. OPEN YOUR HANDS

Slowly open your hands, palms up. Your movement signifies an act of surrender and your willingness to accept life as it *is*.

5. NOTICE YOUR BODY

As she volleyed a tennis ball, Joelle noticed that she was hitting it *really* hard. She asked her body "Why?" and realized she was angry about a situation at work. By noticing her physical actions, she got in touch with her mental agitation. Then she used exercise to help discharge her feelings.

Take inventory of your body by asking, prayerfully, "What's happening in my gut? Is my stomach tight or relaxed? What sensations are in my chest? My back? My shoulders? What do I feel in my throat? Is my brain chattering?"

6. EXTEND YOURSELF

The psalmist says, "Be strong and take heart, all you who hope in the Lord." One way to affirm your strength is to extend yourself beyond your usual comfort zone. If you've been walking one mile, try walking a mile and a half. Or pick up the pace as you walk your one mile.

7. VARY YOUR EXERCISE

The human body adjusts quickly to any repetitious exercise routine, so if you always do the same workout you'll eventually plateau. When that happens, you no longer get the same benefits. And you may get bored.

Cross-training invigorates your muscles and your mind. Vary your spiritual meditation, too. Each time you exercise, read a different verse of Scripture before you start, then meditate on it as you do your workout.

8. Go Outdoors

Even if you normally exercise indoors, add an outdoor activity now and then. Some people experience God more easily when they're out in nature.

> Nature's peace will flow into you as
> sunshine flows into trees . . . and cares will
> drop off like autumn leaves."[15]

9. Be Patient

Patience is the willingness to be at peace with whatever time it takes to reach a goal. It's true for losing weight. Two pounds a week is best.

It's true for exercise. Champion athletes are patient with themselves as they strive to improve. They're also faithful to their practice.

10. Visualize

Athletes have learned that it makes a telling difference if they visualize beforehand the moves and actions planned for a sporting event. Visualizing can help you, too.

- Visualize yourself getting up in the morning to exercise.

- Visualize yourself making the right moves.

- Visualize how you would act, look and feel if you had more stamina and endurance.

- Visualize yourself relaxing and becoming less stressed.

A yoga instructor I know tells her class to lie down on mats. As she leads them through various movements, she says in a slow, hypnotic voice,

Surrender the weight of your body to gravity.
Let go.
The earth will catch and cradle you.
Now imagine that your spine is a river.
Visualize this river flowing between your head and tailbone.
Drop your chin and lengthen the back of the neck
So the river can course freely through you.
Feel yourself return to your natural state of grace.

As I lay on my mat, listening to her rhythmic cadence, I noticed sensations I was normally too busy to notice. The cool, smooth touch of the wooden floor beneath my out-stretched hand. The sound of my breathing. The ticking of a clock. I began to feel tranquil.

I see myself returning to my natural state of grace. Thank you, God!

DO NOT INSIST ON BEING PERFECT

A well-known track coach discovered that when he encouraged his runners to relax a little and perform at what they considered to be 90 percent, paradoxically they often ran faster.

In all things, we are asked *only* to do our best.

Perfection is in God alone.

Accept that in your eating program and your exercise, you are doing the very best you can *today*. Not last week. Not tomorrow. But *today*.

Leave behind any guilt or blame, and say,

Today, oh Lord, I am content with where I am.

CHAPTER TEN
MAINTAINING A HEALTHY WEIGHT NOW AND FOREVER, AMEN

───────── ◈ ─────────

"Bless me, oh Lord, for I have thinned."

One summer, on a car trip out West, I drove up into the Sangre de Christo mountain range east of Alamosa, Colorado. When Isaiah said, "The hand of the Lord will rest on this mountain" (25:10), he might have been speaking of these mountains, for amazingly, half a dozen monasteries are located in the area, including Christian, Buddhist and Hindu. I planned to visit them.

As I drove up from the broad valley floor, the road grew

increasingly narrower and steeper. I could hear my car engine working overtime. I had just made a hairpin turn when I saw this sign, painted on a rough wooden board: "Drive carefully. Road gets harder."

The sign is a reminder of the problem faced by most people who diet. According to the FDA, 86 percent regain their weight because they stop paying attention to what and how they eat. So keep in mind that we are not finished when we reach a particular weight. Our road may even get a little harder. We need to negotiate carefully the twists and turns of everyday eating.

A PRAYER FOR ONGOING COMMITMENT

Beloved Lord, thank you for bringing me to this place
Of wanting health for my body, mind and soul.
Humbly, I claim,
Through the amazing power of your grace,
Strength to continue the good habits I have fostered.
I commit to
Well-planned meals,
Nutritious snacks,
Moderate portions,
Regular exercise.
I make this commitment in the name of Jesus Christ,
who said, "Is not life more than food?" (Matthew 6:25)
And who promised us, "I myself am the bread of life"
(John 6:35).

First Prayerful Action: Maintain Your Support

Just because you've reached your goal weight is no reason to go it alone. Jesus sent his disciples out two by two to spread the good news. Maintaining support over the long haul is important. It's why I saw non-obese people at a meeting of Overeaters Anonymous and why some weight-loss programs encourage members to attend meetings for several weeks *after* they reach their goal weight.

Keep checking in with your friends, family members or online support group.

And since you've made God a key part of your support, remind yourself not to get lax. Continue daily prayer. Prayer is more than a tool for losing weight or redesigning eating habits; it leads us into spiritual transformation.

A Prayer of Support

Dear Lord, I start my day with gratitude,
Acknowledging life's many gifts.
I offer prayers for all
With whom I share Life's journey,
Especially those who, like me,
Desire to eat in a healthy way.
Give us this day what we need.
To keep us strong
In the face of any temptation, Amen.

SECOND PRAYERFUL ACTION: WATCH!

Avoid falling back into old patterns where you grab a handful of nuts without noticing, or eat the leftovers off your children's plates, or give in to cravings while telling yourself, "It's just this once."

Scripture repeatedly calls on us to "Watch." And "Be aware!"

You may have changed your eating patterns, so you no longer have cravings as often as you used to, but it pays to be careful. Old habits can "tiptoe in on cat's feet." Stress has a way of sneaking up on us.

Mary has maintained her healthy weight for twenty years by setting aside fifteen minutes for morning prayer and then stepping on her bathroom scale. "It's easier to lose three pounds than thirty," she says. She admits she is tempted *not* to step on her scale if she knows she overate the day before, but that's precisely when she makes herself do it. "A daily check-up keeps me honest with myself."

A PRAYER FOR WATCHING

> Dear God,
> Watch with me this day.
> Let me see my world
> Through lenses of
> Compassion,
> Kindness,

Enthusiasm, and
Tolerance.
Help me act—and eat—
In simplicity and moderation,
And if I should falter,
Give me eyes to see,
And the will to change. Amen.

Third Prayerful Action: Exercise!

Maintaining our weight is a straightforward equation: simply use up all the calories we consume each day. Calories left over will be stored as fat. That means our choice is always to exercise more or eat less.

Stanford Medical Center reports that 90 percent of those who lost weight in a regimented program and kept it off continued to exercise. They considered it no hardship because they had learned to enjoy their physical activities.

We want to eat in small bites, and we can also exercise in small bites. A twenty-minute walk three times a week. Lifting eight-pound weights while watching TV. Skipping the elevator for stairs or parking farther away. Best of all is finding some physical sport—like biking or water aerobics or tennis—that you like to do.

A priest friend of mine put it this way, "Every day, pray and play."

AN EXERCISE PRAYER

Thank you, God, for my wondrous body!
Flexible, changeable, moveable, bendable.
Today I commit to staying supple.
I jump, run, turn, dance, walk,
And most of all,
I yield.
My body, my soul, my spirit, my mind,
I yield all to your divine will. Amen.

FOURTH PRAYERFUL ACTION: ADOPT NEW ATTITUDES

I want to quote three women who have learned to re-think their attitudes about eating and have successfully maintained their weight loss for more than a year.

To me, each quote is like an affirming prayer.

"It's not a struggle for me anymore. It's become a way of life."

- You might ask yourself, "How have I changed my way of life?"

- Is there any area that is still a struggle?

- What might you do to address that struggle?

"I don't feel like I'm denying myself. I feel like I'm improving myself."

- Are you feeling positive about your new eating habits?
- Are some foods or situations still hard to relinquish?
- Name and give thanks for your areas of improvement.

"I take responsibility for my choices: in what I do, and in what I eat."

- When we binged or gave into cravings, we were blindly reacting. In what ways have you changed?
- In becoming more responsible for your eating choices, do you feel more empowered in other areas of your life?
- How has prayer helped?

Finally, from Dietrich Bonhoeffer: "God cannot endure a mirthless attitude in which we eat our bread in sorrow, with haste or even with shame. Through our daily meals, He is calling us to rejoice! Keep holiday in the midst of our working day."[16]

A Final Prayer of Rejoicing

Oh Lord, I do rejoice!
I eat food the good earth provides.
I eat in good humor and without sorrow.
I eat my right portion, and

Day by day, I give thanks
For my health and well-being.
Your presence fills me with joy.
Alleluia, Alleluia.

CHAPTER ELEVEN
WHEN ALL IS SAID AND DONE:
ONE-MINUTE PRAYERS

"With God I can, with God I can, with God I can."

Losing weight, maintaining a healthy body and exercising exist within the context of everything else we do each day. In *Grace on the Go: 101 Quick Ways to Pray* the theme is incorporating prayer in your ordinary day by "putting a spiritual spin on the daily tasks you're already doing."

I call them one-minute prayers.

Here are some quick, one-minute prayers for weight-loss situations.

WHEN YOU WAKE UP

As your alarm goes off, say aloud,

This is the day the Lord has made. I awake and am glad.
Mine is the body the Lord has made. I rejoice and am glad.

Commit to living in gratitude for the day and to caring for your body with "right eating."

WHEN YOU'RE TEMPTED TO SKIP BREAKFAST

You're in a hurry, no time to eat. But breakfast is the most important meal of the day. Keep apples and nutritionally sound diet drinks on hand for emergency use and say this prayer:

Oh Lord, though I'm starting my day in a hurry, I take time to break my night's fast in your name. Help me slow down enough to fully appreciate the small miracles in this day.

WHEN YOU STEP ON THE SCALE.

(If you see the number you hoped to see)
Thank you, God. I celebrate eating right.

(If you do not see the number you want)
As we do not live by bread alone, I do not live by numbers

alone. Just be with me today, oh Lord, as I strive to eat more lightly.

When You Bypass the Goodie Table at Work

"I do not pay attention to the desires of the body, but instead, trust in the Lord."

Give your self a mental pat on the back. Appreciate that you controlled your appetite.

When Feeling Bad because You Succumbed to Temptation

Failure is not the same as quitting.
Though I may have failed, I will not quit.
Strengthen me, Lord, as I start again.

When Dining Out

As you bypass a glass of wine and the basket of bread, pray to yourself,

I feed my body what it truly needs when it truly needs it.
I feed my soul with the Bread of Life—You!

When Feeling Ravenous in Mid-afternoon

Prepare yourself for this "low-sugar" moment by keeping healthy snacks available. Eat slowly. Say simply,

I give You thanks.

Recall these words:

"Whoever comes to me will never be hungry

And whoever believes in me will never be thirsty."
(John 6:35)

WHEN LOW-CAL SNACKS ARE NOT AVAILABLE AND YOU'RE TEMPTED TO EAT SOMETHING SWEET AND CALORIC

This is the time to drink eight ounces of water and take a brisk walk, even if all you can do is walk rapidly down the halls to the restroom. As you walk, repeat:

Oh Lord, each time I master one desire, I emerge stronger.
Or say,

All things are possible with God. Help me, help me, help me, Lord.

WHEN GOING TO A PARTY

Remind yourself that party enjoyment is not dependent on food but on interesting conversations with other attendees.

Before you leave home, eat a large tossed salad with non-fat dressing. Or fill yourself with a clear broth soup.

Help me to be a good steward of my body, Lord. Help me learn to have fun without needing to eat.

WHEN PASSING A MIRROR AND GETTING DOWN ON YOURSELF

"Charm is deceitful, and beauty is vain, but a woman who

fears the LORD is to be praised" (Proverbs 31:30). Oh Lord, help me love and accept my self as you love and accept me.

WHEN TEMPTED TO INDULGE IN MOVIE POPCORN

- Buy a "junior" bag and give yourself permission to enjoy.
- Bring with you a 100-calorie snack pack of some food you like.
- Substitute a diet drink for the popcorn.

I can do all things through him who strengthens me. (Philippians 4:13)

WHEN TEMPTED TO GIVE UP YOUR EATING PLAN ALTOGETHER

Oh Lord, like a cat holding on for dear life by its claws, so I hold onto my diet. I feel so precarious. In faith, I cry out to you, do not abandon me. Give me the strength to make it through just one more day.

WHEN ANY TEMPTATION STRIKES

Oh Lord, I recall these words from James: "Submit yourselves therefore to God. Resist the devil, and he will flee from you" (James: 4:7).

And I say, in the words Jesus gave us to pray:

"Deliver me from evil.

For yours is the kingdom, the power, and the glory, forever and ever, Amen.

NOTES

1. *The New Scofield Study Bible* (New York: Oxford University Press, 1984).

2. Ibid.

3. Macrina Wiederkehr, "Sessions of Your Heart," quoted in Virginia Ann Froehle, *Loving Yourself More: 101 Meditations for Women* (Notre Dame, IN: Ave Maria Press, 2007), 31.

4. Thomas À Kempis, *The Imitation of Christ*, in *Devotional Classics*, edited by Richard Foster and James Bryan Smith (San Francisco: HarperSanFrancisco, 1989), 186.

5. Edward Hays, *Prayer Notes to a Friend* (Leavenworth, KS: Forest of Peace Publishing, 2002), 86.

6. Stephen R. Covey, in Stephen R. Covey, A. Roger Merrill, Rebecca R. Merrill, *First Things First* (New

York: Simon and Schuster, 1994), 59. Emphasis added.

7. David Adam, *Celtic Daily Prayers: Prayers and Readings from the Northumbria Community* (New York: Harper One, 2002), 146.

8. www.leahwolfsong.net.

9. Kempis, *The Imitation of Christ*, 185.

10. Fr. Edward Hays, Daily Personal Prayers.

11. Kempis, *The Imitation of Christ*, 186.

12. Hays, *Prayer Notes to a Friend*, 30.

13. Ibid.

14. www.dancemagazine.com.

15. John Muir, *Our National Parks* (Boston/New York: Houghton Mifflin & Company, 1901), 56.

16. Dietrich Bonhoeffer, quoted in *The World Treasury of Religious Quotations*, edited by Ralph L. Woods (New York: Garland Books, 1966), 516.

RESOURCES

BOOKS

Anderson, Matthew. *The Prayer Diet*. New York: Citadel Press, 2001.

Bartocci, Barbara. *Meditation in Motion*. Notre Dame, IN: Sorin Books, 2002.

Colbert, Don. *What Would Jesus Eat?* Nashville: Thomas Nelson Publishers, 2002.

Coyle, Neva, and Marie Chapian. *Free to Be Thin*. Minneapolis: Bethany House, 1993.

Lerner, Ben. *Body By God: The Owner's Manual for Maximized Living*. Nashville: Thomas Nelson Publishers, 2003.

McGraw, Phil. *The Ultimate Weight Solution: The Seven Keys to Weight Loss Freedom*. New York: The Free Press/Simon and Schuster, 2003.

Moran, Victoria. *Fat, Broke, and Lonely No More!: Your Personal Solution to Overeating, Overspending, and Looking for Love in All the Wrong Places.* New York: HarperOne, 2007.

———. *Fit From Within: 101 simple Secrets to Change Your Body and Your Life, Starting Today and Lasting Forever.* Chicago: Contemporary Books, 2002.

Yphantides, Nick, with Mike Yorkey. *My Big Fat Greek Diet.* Nashville: Thomas Nelson Publishers, 2004.

ONLINE RESOURCES

Below are ranked web sites for dieters as compiled by the *Consumer Reports* Web Watch and the Health Improvement Institute. (Sites within a rating category are not ranked higher or lower than others in that same category.)

Excellent:
- Aetna InteliHealth, www.intelihealth.com
- MayoClinic.com
- MedicineNet.com (a WebMD company)

Very Good:
- National Institutes of Health, www.nih.gov
- WebMD, www.webmd.com

Good:
- eDiets.com
- RealAge, www.RealAge.com
- WeightWatchers.com

Fair:
- About Health & Fitness, www.healthandfitness.com
- MSN Health & Fitness, www.healthmsn.com
- The Biggest Loser Club, www.thebiggestloserclub.com
- The Sonoma Diet, www.SonomaDiet.com
- The South Beach Diet, www.SouthBeachDiet.com
- Yahoo! Health, www.YahooHealth.com

Poor:
- AOL Health, www.AOLHealth.com
- Healthology, www.Healthology.com
- www.Prevention.com
- www.QualityHealth.com
- TrimLife, www.TrimLife.com

OTHER ONLINE RESOURCES INCLUDE THE FOLLOWING:

This is not intended to be a full list of online resources. Consider each of these a "starting point" in your own research.

www.firstplace.org

A Christ-centered, interdenominational health program for men and women incorporating Bible study, prayer, balanced eating, and exercise plan.

www.healthyweightforum.com

A free, independent peer education-based forum offering

support, motivation, recipes, and fellowship for those who want to reach and maintain healthy weight.

www.mydietbuddy.com

A free, secure website where you can connect with one or more fellow dieters based on criteria you establish. Recommended by *Woman's World* magazine.

www.overeatersanonymous.com

www.oa.org

Addresses physical, emotional and spiritual well-being for compulsive overeaters based on the 12-step program. It is not a religious organization and does not promote any particular diet.

Also check your local white pages for the Overeaters Anonymous telephone number.

Call the World Service Office at (213) 542-8363.

www.Weighdown.com

A nondenominational, faith-based program for men and women. There is a fee for materials.

www.WeightLossBuddy.com.

A free, independent website where you can find a diet buddy, recipes, and support.

POCKET GUIDES TO PRAYER FOR PEOPLE ON THE GO!
THE GRACE ON THE GO SERIES FROM BARBARA BARTOCCI

Grace on the Go:
101 Quick Ways
to Pray

Grace on the Go
for Compassionate
Caregivers

Available from Morehouse Publishing
An imprint of Church Publishing Incorporated
www.churchpublishing.org
800-877-0012

Grace on the Go
for Determined
Dieters

Grace on the Go
for New Moms